T0021109

@RosenTeenTalk

SUICIDE

Xina M. Uhl

ROSEN PUBLISHING

Published in 2024 by The Rosen Publishing Group, Inc.
2544 Clinton Street, Buffalo, NY 14224

Copyright © 2024 by The Rosen Publishing Group, Inc.

All rights reserved. No part of this book may be reproduced in any form without permission in writing from the publisher, except by a reviewer.

First Edition

Editor: Greg Roza
Designer: Rachel Rising

Photo Credits: Cover, pp. 1, 3, 45 Ollyy/Shutterstock.com; Cover, pp. 1-48 Vitya_M/Shutterstock.com; Cover, p. 28 Cosmic_Design/Shutterstock.com; pp. 3, 5 Dean Drobot/Shutterstock.com; pp. 3, 11 fizkes/Shutterstock.com; pp. 3, 19 Katarzyna Hurova/Shutterstock.com; pp. 3, 25 Prixel Creative/Shutterstock.com; pp. 3, 33 Bernardo Emanuelle/Shutterstock.com; pp. 3, 39 Daniel M Ernst/Shutterstock.com; p. 6 https://www.cdc.gov/suicide/suicide-data-statistics.html; p. 7 olesea vetrila/Shutterstock.com; p. 9 Atstock Productions/Shutterstock.com; p. 13 Nikodash/Shutterstock.com; p. 14 Tartila/Shutterstock.com; p. 15 KMarsh/Shutterstock.com; p. 16 Pixel-Shot/Shutterstock.com; p. 17 Featureflash Photo Agency/Shutterstock.com; p. 21 Kathy Hutchins/Shutterstock.com; p. 23 monticello/Shutterstock.com; p. 27 fast-stock/Shutterstock.com; p. 29 Chokniti-Studio/Shutterstock.com; p. 31 SeventyFour/Shutterstock.com; p. 32 mspoint/Shutterstock.com; p. 35 Rawpixel.com/Shutterstock.com; p. 37 SynthEx/Shutterstock.com; p. 38 Lightspring/Shutterstock.com; p. 41 LADO/Shutterstock.com; p. 42 Jane Semina/Shutterstock.com; p. 43 Jacek Chabraszewski/Shutterstock.com.

Some of the images in this book illustrate individuals who are models. The depictions do not imply actual situations or events.

Library of Congress Cataloging-in-Publication Data

Names: Uhl, Xina M., author.
Title: Suicide / Xina M. Uhl.
Description: [New York City] : Rosen Publishing, [2024] | Series:
    @Rosenteentalk | Includes index.
Identifiers: LCCN 2023009864 (print) | LCCN 2023009865 (ebook) | ISBN
    9781499469431 (library binding) | ISBN 9781499469424 (paperback) | ISBN
    9781499469448 (ebook)
Subjects: LCSH: Suicide--Juvenile literature. | Teenagers--Suicidal
    behavior--Juvenile literature.
Classification: LCC HV6546 .U35 2024 (print) | LCC HV6546 (ebook) | DDC
    362.280835--dc23/eng/20230323
LC record available at https://lccn.loc.gov/2023009864
LC ebook record available at https://lccn.loc.gov/2023009865

Manufactured in the United States of America

CPSIA Compliance Information: Batch #CSRYA24. For Further Information contact Rosen Publishing at 1-800-237-9932.

Find us on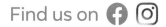

CONTENTS

Chapter 1

Under My Mask

My name is Andre. I am popular at my high school. Sports trophies line my shelves. My friends thought I was happy. But I cried a lot, and couldn't get out of bed. To cope, or deal with these feelings, I drank hard liquor and hid the bottles. Other times I didn't sleep, and had a lot of energy.

My parents took me to a doctor. She said I have **bipolar II**, and I needed to take **medicine** every day. I took it for a while. But then I stopped.

I managed until my dad found the empty bottles. He didn't yell at me. But I knew he was disappointed.

I felt awful. I opened my bedroom window. We lived three stories up. On **impulse**, I jumped.

> You can't tell what a person is thinking or how they feel just by looking at them. We all have thoughts we hide from others.

FACTS ABOUT SUICIDE

Suicide, or death by taking one's own life, is a major problem in the United States. The number of people who died by suicide increased 30 percent from 2000 to 2018, but dropped in 2019 and 2020. Still, almost 46,000 people died by suicide in 2020.

From 2000 to 2018, suicides rose quickly. They came down in 2019 and 2020, but they are still too high.

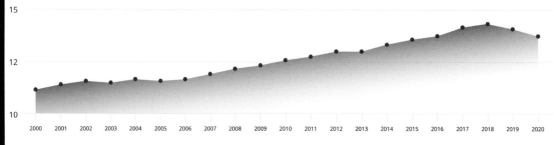

15

12

10

2000 2001 2002 2003 2004 2005 2006 2007 2008 2009 2010 2011 2012 2013 2014 2015 2016 2017 2018 2019 2020

Age-adjusted rates per 100,000

Suicide affects people of all ages. It can affect all gender identities. People from all social classes die by suicide. People from all races do too.

Suicide affects more than just the person involved. It affects their family and friends too. It also affects the whole community. The medical costs are high too. This figure reached about a half billion dollars in 2019.

Poor **mental** health can result in suicide. But in 2016 more than half of those who died by suicide did *not* have a mental health condition. Clearly, suicide is a big problem.

But there is help.

- One person dies by suicide every 11 minutes.
- In 2020,
  - about 12 million Americans seriously thought about suicide
  - about 3 million Americans planned to kill themselves
  - about 1.2 million Americans attempted suicide

WHO IS AT GREATEST RISK?

While suicide can happen to anyone, some people are at greater risk. They are members of certain groups:

MALES—In 2020, males were four times as likely to die by suicide as females (although females are more likely to *attempt* suicide).

AMERICAN INDIANS—American Indians have the highest rate of suicide. Most of these deaths were people younger than 44 years old. The next highest group is white people. But American Indian suicides are about 20 percent higher.

VETERANS—People who have served in the military make up a little less than 14 percent of adult suicides.

PEOPLE FROM RURAL AREAS—Job loss, **poverty**, and family problems may affect the number of deaths by suicide for people in **rural** areas.

LGBTQ+ POPULATION—In high school, **LGBTQ+** individuals die by suicide at almost four times the rate of others.

Age also matters. People 75 and older have the highest rate of suicide. People aged 35 to 64 years make up almost half of all the suicide deaths each year. Teenagers and young adults ages 10 to 24 make up 14 percent of all suicides.

LGBTQ+ people have increased risk of dying by suicide. This risk is worse during youth.

Chapter 2

A Deadly Impulse

My parents and I don't talk much. They never seem to agree with what I want to do. In high school, I spent a lot of time with my boyfriend, Jose. We had grown so close, and I felt like I could tell him anything. So, when Jose broke up with me, I was more than sad. I felt like there was no help for me. I felt like there was no one I could talk to.

One night I went to the medicine cabinet. *If I take the whole bottle of my dad's pain pills,* I thought, *everything will be over . . . But what would my parents do?*

Then I woke up my mom and dad and told them what I was thinking.

It can be hard to talk to others about our problems. But there's no need to suffer in silence.

WHY DO PEOPLE DIE BY SUICIDE?

Many reasons can cause someone to die by suicide. They can include problems with health, money, family, and more.

MENTAL ILLNESS—**Depression** robs people of joy and hope. **Eating disorders** make life a struggle. Other mental illnesses may not be discovered or treated in time.

TRAUMA—**Trauma** can come from bullying, physical (bodily) abuse, war, or other sources. Abuse is treating a person in a harmful or harsh way.

DRUGS OR ALCOHOL—The use of illegal drugs often goes along with suicide. It is hard to think clearly when using drugs and alcohol regularly.

CHRONIC (ONGOING) ILLNESS—Living with an illness like cancer makes life harder. Ongoing pain is also a problem.

PEOPLE PROBLEMS—Being bullied or not getting along with family can cause **stress**.

Perhaps the biggest reason for suicide is a loss of hope. Feeling like things cannot get better can be dangerous, or unsafe. This can crowd out the good things in life. It can also make a person feel like life can never change. A good attitude, or way of thinking, can keep you alive, but sometimes that's hard to do.

Divorce or other family problems can bring great stress into people's lives.

INNER PAIN

Often, people who die by suicide have planned out the act. They have thought about how it will take place. They have decided where and when it will occur. But this is not always true. Sometimes, people will attempt suicide on impulse. Of those who survived, or lived through, suicide attempts, studies show:

- Almost half thought about attempting suicide for less than 10 minutes before they acted
- Most did not suffer from major depression
- Many had just had a fight with a family member or other loved one

Dr. David Rosen has studied suicide survivors. He said: " . . . none of them had truly wanted to die. They had wanted their inner pain to stop."

Very few people who jump from the Golden Gate Bridge in San Francisco survive. Kevin Hines is one who survived. He remembers his hands coming off the bridge railing. At that moment, he thought, "My God, what have I just done?"

Building barriers, such as walls and fences, can keep people from dying by suicide by jumping from tall buildings and bridges. Some bridges feature signs like this one to reach out to people who might be thinking of dying by suicide.

Life is Worth Living

Lifeline
24-Hour Hotline
Phone Ahead

Or Call
1-800-273-TALK
(8255)

CELEBRITY SUICIDES

Being rich and famous is not enough to keep some from dying by suicide. People in the spotlight may seem to have it all. But they could be suffering as well.

Stephen "tWitch" Boss, the DJ on the *Ellen* TV talk show, is one who proved this to be true. The popular dancer seemed happy and joyful. He smiled on television. tWitch's death caused actor and filmmaker Tyler Perry to talk about his own suicide attempts. He said:

- Reach out to someone
- Ask for help
- Know that life gets better

Treatments for suicidal thoughts exist. Even though life can get hard, don't give up. If Perry had died by suicide, he has said he would have missed out on "the best part of my life." He has also said:

- Life can be filled with love and joy.
- "Do not let the darkness stop you."
- Keep going on—trust that life will get better.

Tyler Perry is well-known as the creator of the *Madea* comedies.

Chapter 3

CAUSES OF SUICIDE

Mental health has to do with our emotions and thoughts. It also involves how we interact with one another. Mental health includes:

- How we think
- How we feel
- How we act
- How we treat ourselves
- How we treat others
- The choices we make

Mental health can be affected by:
- Our **genes**
- Things that have happened to us
- Family history

When people have a problem with mental health, they may feel **ashamed**. Many people feel a stigma, or a sense of public shame, by it. This can make them unwilling to get treated. We can all work to reduce the stigma of mental illnesses.

Depression can be treated. Talk **therapy** is often used to treat it. So is medication. That's why it is important to see a doctor for depression.

We all have feelings of sadness every now and again. But depression is when these feelings last at least two weeks and get in the way of everyday activities.

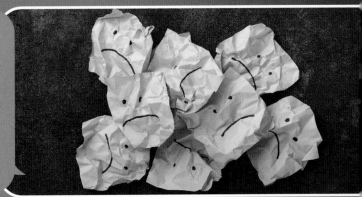

SIGNS OF DEPRESSION

Depression is a very common illness. It is a mood **disorder**. Symptoms (or signs) are:

- Feeling sad constantly
- Loss of energy
- Weight change
- Problems with sleep
- Loss of joy
- Feeling worthless
- Thoughts of death or suicide

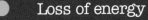

DEALING WITH ANXIETY

Everyone experiences anxiety at some point. It's normal to experience worry over family problems, money, or health. When anxiety does not go away it can become a disorder. Anxiety disorders affect school, work, and relationships. Symptoms are:

- Feeling on-edge or restless
- Difficulty, or problems with, thinking
- Irritability (quick to anger)
- Uncontrollable worry
- Sleep problems
- Fatigue (tiredness)

Some people have panic attacks. Symptoms include:
- Sweating
- Racing heart

- Trembling (shaking)
- Chest pain
- Dread (great fear)

About 19 percent of U.S. adults have an anxiety disorder and 7 percent of children experience anxiety issues. Some people who deal with anxiety attempt suicide. This is why it is important to be seen by a doctor.

Reynolds has been open about his struggles with anxiety. Here, he poses with his star on Hollywood Boulevard in Los Angeles.

CELEBRITY ANXIETY

Actor Ryan Reynolds has suffered from anxiety since childhood. To keep from angering his father, he tried to keep the house very clean. He often found himself waking up in the night with anxiety and worry.

Now, in his 40s, Reynolds uses **meditation** to help settle himself down. Acting, especially comedy, also relieves his anxiety. It allows him to change his nervous energy into a fun career, or job.

SUBSTANCE ABUSE AND SUICIDE: A STRONG LINK

Studies tell us that the majority of suicides involve drugs, alcohol, or both. Drugs can be prescribed, or ordered, by a doctor. Examples of prescribed medicine include:

OPIOIDS—A family of painkillers

BENZODIAZEPINES—Make the brain less sensitive to **stimulus**

ANTIDEPRESSANTS—Relieve feelings of depression

Some legal drugs can be bought without a prescription. An example of over-the-counter medicine is acetaminophen (sometimes called Tylenol).

One study, covering the years 2005 to 2007, showed that females were more likely to die from alcohol or drug overdose than males. In fact, females were four times more likely than males.

Legal drugs can be just as dangerous as illegal drugs.

988: A HELPFUL RESOURCE

What do you do if you need emergency (or sudden) medical services, fire, or police? You call 911.

But did you know you can get emergency mental health care by calling or texting 988? This care involves being connected to a trained counselor. You can call this lifeline if you or a loved one are:

- Thinking of suicide
- Feeling lonely or sad
- Having relationship problems
- Using drugs or drinking too much
- Feeling overwhelmed, or like too much is happening all at once

Chapter 4

SIGNS, SYMPTOMS, AND GETTING HELP

Some suicides occur without warning. That is the truth. But other suicides may have warning signs. We should train ourselves to listen to others, and be aware if we hear people saying things like:

- "I want to kill myself."
- "The pain is too much."
- "I feel trapped."
- "There's no reason to live."
- "I'm a **burden**."
- "There's no hope."
- "Soon this will all be over."

Those who are thinking of dying by suicide don't always talk about it. Instead, they may have changes in their moods. Notice when people act in out of the ordinary ways such as showing:

- Anxiety
- Depression
- Anger
- Feeling ashamed
- Feeling irritated
- Despair (feeling there is no hope)
- Loss of interest in things that used to provide joy

People's behavior can also change. This can happen quickly. Look out for:

- Avoiding others
- A change in sleep habits
- New or increased use of drugs or alcohol
- Giving away things
- Saying goodbye to people

If you notice any warning signs, take them seriously. Tell a parent or trusted adult. Or call or text a lifeline like 988.

Sometimes we see people as we want them to be, not as how they are.

GETTING HELP

What if you feel suicidal right now? Take these steps as soon as possible:

STEP #1: MAKE A PROMISE NOT TO DO ANYTHING FOR NOW.

You may be in a lot of pain, but you need distance between thought and action. Tell yourself: "I will give myself a 24-hour waiting period." Do not do anything impulsive during that time. Or, change the time to a week.

STEP #2: DO NOT TAKE DRUGS OR DRINK ALCOHOL.

Drugs or alcohol can make suicidal thoughts worse.

STEP #3: MAKE YOUR HOME SAFE.

Get rid of things you could use to hurt yourself, such as pills, knives, or firearms. If you can't get rid of them, go somewhere safe.

STEP #4: TELL SOMEONE.

Find someone you trust and tell them what you are thinking. If the first person doesn't take you seriously, tell someone else. You can always call the lifeline 988 for quick help.

STEP #5: REMEMBER—YOU WILL GET THROUGH THIS.

Others who feel like you're feeling now manage to survive these feelings. You can too.

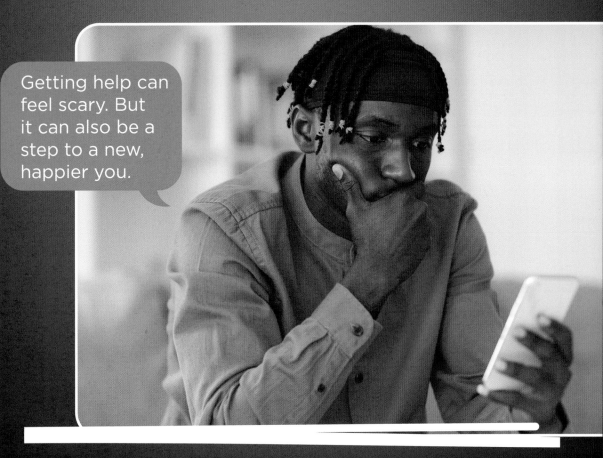

Getting help can feel scary. But it can also be a step to a new, happier you.

DON'T MAKE MY MISTAKE

To all people thinking of suicide,

One night in high school I took a whole bottle of acetaminophen. I said goodbye to my friends earlier that day. They told my parents and I ended up in the hospital. Then I had to take a gross medicine that made me throw up. I remember seeing my parents crying and praying. I had never seen my dad cry before. People love you more than you know.

Now I have two pet bunnies. What would they do without me? They keep me going. So does therapy. I have a plan now to get help if I have thoughts of suicide again. It includes people I can call and things I can do to feel better.

Love,
Amy 💕

Pets can be a great source of comfort. They are a responsibility too. They depend on us to take care of them.

WHAT HAPPENS IN TREATMENT?

During an emergency, people facing suicide may need to go to a hospital. What if you are having suicidal thoughts, but aren't in a **crisis**? Then you may need outpatient treatment, meaning you visit a medical building for treatment but do not stay there. This may include:

TALK THERAPY—Talk therapy takes place between you and a therapist. Together, you figure out what made you feel suicidal. You also learn skills to deal with strong emotions, or feelings.

MEDICATION—There are a number of medicines that may help you feel better. A doctor will tell you what's best for you.

ADDICTION TREATMENT—If you have a drug or alcohol **addiction**, treatment can help. Special addiction treatment programs and self-help groups are available too.

FAMILY SUPPORT—While families can be a source of great support, they can also be a source of struggle. When family members are included in your treatment, they can help the therapist understand what you're going through. Together, you and your family can learn to better cope and communicate, or talk together.

Self-help groups, including 12-step groups for addiction, can be a source of healing. You may be helped by hearing other people's stories. You might help someone else by telling your story.

Chapter 5

HELPING OTHERS IN NEED

What do you do if you are worried that a loved one may be in danger of suicide? It depends on the situation. If someone needs emergency help, don't leave them alone. Keep them away from deadly things, such as firearms and drugs. If someone is not in immediate danger, then have an open and honest discussion about your concerns.

- Talk to the person in private
- Tell them you care about them
- Ask directly if they are thinking about suicide
- Listen to them
- Tell them to talk to their doctor
- Offer your support

You can't make someone seek help. But you can reassure them to do so. You can help them find a therapist or support group. You can give them a crisis number. You can also offer to go with them to their appointment, or meetings. But you do NOT want to:

- Argue about the value of life
- Minimize, or belittle, their problems
- Give advice

Being a source of support for a suicidal person can be hard. It may make you feel afraid and helpless. Remember that you can ask for help for yourself too.

Being a friend is so important for those who are thinking about suicide. You may not know what to say, but just being there can be a big deal.

WHEN THE WORST HAPPENS

When someone we care about has died by suicide, it is a terrible shock. It is natural to wonder why. We may feel:

- Numb, or without feelings
- Very emotional
- Unable to think
- Anxious
- Unable to sleep

If you are supporting someone who has suffered a loss by suicide, it can be hard to know what to say. It is always okay to say: "I don't know what to say. But I am here for you."

Do NOT say: "I understand what you're going through." Because chances are, you don't.

A Helpful Resource

The **Alliance** of Hope for Suicide Loss Survivors, allianceof-hope.org, is a group created by suicide survivors, *for* suicide survivors. You can find helpful **forums**, resources, and support.

Family members and friends are at higher risk for suicide themselves when someone they know has died by suicide.

MYTHS AND FACTS ABOUT SUICIDE

MYTH: Discussing suicide increases the rate of suicides.

FACT: It's just the opposite. Talking about suicide reduces suicidal thoughts. Asking a person if they are considering suicide can help them get treatment.

MYTH: People talk about suicide to get attention.

FACT: People who consider suicide may not see the future. Always take people seriously if they talk about hurting themselves.

MYTH: Suicide can't be stopped.

FACT: Suicide can be stopped, but it's **unpredictable**. Suicide has many causes including genes, mental illnesses, and family factors. Treatment saves lives.

MYTH: People who take their own lives are selfish.

FACT: People die by suicide because they are in pain and feel hopeless. They may also have a mental illness.

MYTH: Barriers to bridges and storing firearms safely to prevent suicides don't work.

FACT: Adding bridge barriers and limiting firearm access does decrease suicide chances. This is because many suicide attempts are impulsive decisions.

One myth is that people talk about suicide to get attention. This is not true.

Chapter 6

HEALING FROM SUICIDAL THOUGHTS

It may be tempting, or appealing, to try to deal with suicidal thoughts on your own. That is dangerous. You need help in order to overcome the problems linked to suicidal thinking. Make sure that you:

ATTEND YOUR APPOINTMENTS—This is serious business. Don't skip therapy or doctor's appointments. Trust the experts, not your own judgment.

TAKE YOUR MEDICINE—Skipping medication prescribed by a doctor may cause suicidal feelings to come back. Suddenly stopping an antidepressant or other medication may cause you to experience **withdrawal**.

LEARN ABOUT YOUR CONDITION—Finding out more information, or facts, about your condition can be helpful. It can **empower** you. It can also move you to stick to your treatment plan.

PAY ATTENTION TO WARNING SIGNS—Your doctor or therapist can help you learn what **triggers** suicidal feelings. Decide what steps to take ahead of time. When you spot the danger signs you are prepared to act. Always let your doctor or therapist know if you notice any changes in how you feel.

Doctors and therapists are professionals who can help you. Follow their advice and allow them to help you.

COPING WITH HARMFUL URGES

If you have had thoughts of suicide in the past, they may return. Make a plan so you know what to do in the moment. It may help to make a written agreement with someone else when you don't have the best judgment. Other ideas are:

- Be upfront with your therapist about any suicidal thoughts.
- Have a family member or friend give you your medications as prescribed if you are worried that you might overdose, or take enough to cause lasting damage or death.

Attend a support group. You can find them online at **afsp.org/find-a-support-group.**

If you are in crisis, another 24/7 helpline can be reached by texting "home" to 741741.

MANAGING YOUR STRESS

Life has its ups and downs. By learning ways to identify and manage stress you can head off thoughts of suicide. Ask yourself:

- Am I irritable?
- Do small events upset me easily?
- Am I isolating, or withdrawing, myself from others?
- Am I feeling worthless?
- Am I sleeping well?
- How is my eating?
- Is it hard to breathe?
- How is my energy level?

Your answers to these questions may reveal, or show, that you are more stressed than you realize. If that's the case, there are things you can do:

- Relax by taking a walk, playing a video game, taking a bath, or chatting with a friend.
- Make sure you are eating right. Good nutrition helps you deal with stress.
- Reduce anxiety by 50 percent with exercise, or movement that increases breathing and heart rate.
- Regular sleep is key to good mental health.
- Manage your time and schedule, or daily plan.
- Don't try to do too many things at one time; this can become overwhelming.
- Don't ignore your stress. Find ways to defuse, or lessen, it.

Movement and nature go hand in hand. Spending time outside can improve your mental health while you enjoy yourself.

Chapter 7

A Second Chance

Jumping out a window did not kill me. I woke up in the hospital, covered in bandages. My parents cried when they saw me. I spent five days in a **coma**, and had only a 40 percent chance of living. It was more than a year before I could walk again. My recovery was awful.

I began to take my bipolar II seriously. I took my medicine. I went to a therapist. I talked to my therapist about my drinking. I joined a 12-step group and dealt with my alcohol problem.

Before, I thought I was the only person to have suicidal thoughts, but that's not true. Now, I tell my story to other people with thoughts of suicide. It helps all of us. I still have struggles, but I'm glad to be alive.

These days, my smile is real. Telling my story has helped me heal from suicidal thoughts.

GLOSSARY

addiction: A powerful and harmful need to often have something, such as a drug, or do something, such as gambling.

alliance: A union between people, groups, or countries.

ashamed: Feeling shame or blame.

bipolar II: A mental health condition which involves major mood swings and often longer depressive episodes.

burden: Something hard to take on or carry.

coma: A long sleeplike state caused by disease, injury, or poison.

crisis: An unstable or difficult situation.

depression: A mental health condition in which a person feels very sad, hopeless, and unimportant and is often unable to do basic tasks because of this.

disorder: A condition that affects the body (physical) or the mind (mental).

eating disorder: One of several mental health conditions including anorexia nervosa and bulimia that involve a major change in eating behaviors.

empower: To give power to someone.

forum: A place or meeting where ideas are exchanged.

genes: Tiny parts of a cell that are passed along from parent to child and that decide specific features in the child, such as eye color.

impulse: A quick feeling or desire to take action.

LGBTQ+: Abbreviation for lesbian, gay, bisexual, transgender, and queer/questioning. The plus symbol indicates that other groups may be included.

medicine: A drug taken to make a sick person well.

meditation: The process or activity of spending time in quiet thought.

mental: Having to do with the mind.

poverty: The state of being poor.

rural: Having to do with the country or life in the country.

stimulus: Something in the world around us that acts to partly change a bodily activity.

stress: A state of concern, worry, or feeling nervous.

therapy: A way of dealing with problems that make people's bodies and minds feel better. A therapist is someone who helps with a certain physical or mental illness.

trauma: An experience that causes serious distress.

treatment: Steps used to change or improve something.

trigger: Something that begins or stirs up a feeling or reply.

unpredictable: Unable to predict (guess) that something will happen.

withdrawal: The physical and mental problems that happen when a person stops taking a drug.

INDEX